AN B

Did You
CHESTE

A MISCELLANY

Compiled by Julia Skinner

With particular reference to the work of Clive Hardy

THE FRANCIS FRITH COLLECTION

www.francisfrith.com

First published in the United Kingdom in 2009 by The Francis Frith Collection®

This edition published exclusively for Bradwell Books in 2012
For trade enquiries see: www.bradwellbooks.com or tel: 0800 834 920
ISBN 978-1-84589-399-6

British Library Cataloguing in Publication Data

Did You Know? Chesterfield - A Miscellany
Compiled by Julia Skinner
With particular reference to the work of Clive Hardy

The Francis Frith Collection
Oakley Business Park,
Wylye Road, Dinton,
Wiltshire SP3 5EU
Tel: +44 (0) 1722 716 376
Email: info@francisfrith.co.uk
www.francisfrith.com

Printed and bound in Malaysia
Contains material sourced from responsibly managed forests

Front Cover: **CHESTERFIELD, STEPHENSON PLACE 1914** 67563p

The colour-tinting is for illustrative purposes only, and is not intended to be historically accurate

CONTENTS

INTRODUCTION

Despite having its origins in Roman times, Chesterfield's modern development was due to the fact that it lay in the midst of a busy coal-mining district, which in turn attracted other industries, including Stavely and Sheepbridge ironworks and Markham & Co.

In the 1960s Chesterfield Borough Council, like many others around Britain, wanted to sweep away the town's old buildings and redevelop the area in the name of progress. It planned that the Market Place, Market Hall, New Square and the Shambles would be consigned to history, and in their place would rise a covered shopping centre spreading over five acres, topped off with a five-storey office block which would come with planning permission to go up to eleven storeys. When local people realised what was intended for their town centre they strenuously objected - and the council found itself on the receiving end of the biggest backlash in the town's history. By the time of a public enquiry in December 1967 no less that 204 objections had been lodged, and the inquiry sat for 32 days. The Civic Society stated that perfectly sound buildings were being needlessly pulled down, and that the plan 'showed a lack of understanding of the aesthetic and symbolic value of buildings enduring in their original setting'. Despite this, demolition work started. The Mansfield Vaults and the 'King and Miller' were among the casualties, and a demolition order on the listed Quaker Meeting House in Saltergate was granted conditionally in 1973 so that a multi-storey car park could be built.

In 1977 there was a complete change of plan. It was suggested that the Market Hall be restored and reconstructed with a new western section, that original shop frontages be retained where practical, and that the Shambles be rehabilitated. The Market Hall was officially reopened in November 1981, and the open market now operates three days a week, drawing shoppers in from miles around.

Happily for those concerned with the town's heritage, attitudes have now changed to redevelopment in the town. Since the 1980s Chesterfield has gained an international reputation for conservation, and any proposed redevelopment within the town's conservation area must be sympathetic to its surroundings. Chesterfield may have few outstanding buildings, but the half-timbered revival shops of Knifesmithgate, the medieval layout of the Shambles and the area around the Market Place with its Market Hall and associated open market all come together to give the town character.

CHESTERFIELD, MARKET HALL 1896 37802

DERBYSHIRE
WORDS AND PHRASES

'Ah've bin up all naight wee a badly rabbit' - I've had a sleepless night.

'Be said' - that's enough, end of conversation.

'Clammed' - very hungry.

'Caded' - spoilt.

'Causey' - pavement.

'Cob' - a bread roll.

'The Dogshelf' - the floor.

'Mardy' - peevish, childish, easily upset.

'Mizzle' - very light, misty rain.

'Put wood int th' ole!' - Shut the door!

'Scratin'' - crying.

'Teggies' - teeth, especially of children.

Leash Fen, or Leys Fen, on moorland west of Chesterfield is believed to be the site of a deserted town, possibly dating back to the Iron Age, which is recalled in an old rhyme:

> *When Chesterfield was gorse and broom*
> *Leash Fen was a market town.*
> *Now Chesterfield is a market town,*
> *Leash Fen is but gorse and broom.*

HAUNTED CHESTERFIELD

Once upon a time there was a house on the site of the present Town Hall, which was called Rosehill. In about 1830, when the tenant was a Mr James Ashwell, the bells used for calling servants to individual rooms developed the habit of ringing by themselves. Even the installation of a new bell system failed to stop these strange happenings, and the bells even rang after the wires had been cut. No explanation was ever found.

The house and garden at Ringwood Hall Hotel at Brimington is said to be haunted by the ghost of a lady in Victorian clothing.

There are several ghost stories associated with coal mines in the Chesterfield area:
Markham Colliery was said to be haunted by the ghost of a former deputy who appeared in a flooded areas of the mine where drainage pumps needed to be activated. Cotgrave Pit was roamed by a phantom that walked through walls to frighten the miners, and the ghost of a man who had recently died was seen in the mineshafts at Williamthorpe Colliery.

Bolsover Castle near Chesterfield is said to be haunted by two female ghosts. One is a lady in a white dress who roams the grounds, and the other is a woman seen in the kitchen, who appears carrying a baby which she carefully puts down in the fireplace.

North Wingfield church is said to be haunted by the shade of a woman carrying young children, usually seen in the winter.

One of the most haunted buildings in the Chesterfield area is Sutton Scarsdale Hall, where the mysterious phenomena which have been reported include floating dismembered body parts, the unexplained sound of footsteps and the strong scent of tobacco, and eerie wails and screams. Moving shadows in the cellar have been filmed by paranormal investigators, and a sobbing lady is said to roam between the hall and the church.

CHESTERFIELD MISCELLANY

Chesterfield's history goes back to Roman times, when a fort was established here which was garrisoned until at least AD350. The fort was one of a chain of military installations, on the road between Derby and York. There were a number of small forts strung out along the roads of Cheshire and Derbyshire, securing lines of communication for the legionary bases at Chester and York, policing the local natives and regulating the movement of salt and copper ore from Cheshire and lead from the Derbyshire mines.

Holy Trinity Church was built in 1838 on land given for the purpose by William, 6th Duke of Devonshire. Restoration work in the 1880s included the strengthening of the roof timbers and building an organ loft. The fine embattled tower of the church houses a clock and one bell. When Holy Trinity became an ecclesiastical parish in its own right in 1841 it included the West Park area, though this was taken away when the boundaries were adjusted in 1908.

At the Peace of Wedmore in AD878 between the Danes (or Vikings) and the Anglo-Saxon King Alfred the Great, the two sides agreed to split the country into two areas of control. The Danes were allowed to settle in the Danelaw where Danish laws, not Anglo-Saxon, were followed. Associated with Chesterfield is the wapentake of Scarsdale, and this is an echo of the time when this area was part of the Danelaw. 'Wapentake' literally means 'show of weapons' - the Danish way of voting at public meetings was by holding a sword or spear aloft, which was more colourful than simply having a show of hands!

The first written reference to Chesterfield, then called Cestrefeud, dates back to AD955.

CHESTERFIELD, HOLY TRINITY CHURCH 1914 67567

CHESTERFIELD, KNIFESMITHGATE c1955 C83014

Photograph C83014 (above) shows the view down Knifesmithgate, one of Chesterfield's oldest streets, towards the distinctive spire of the parish church. The name of the street probably derives from the medieval cutlers who once traded here, but it is also possible that the street was named after the Knivesmith family. The black and white mock-Tudor half-timbered shops were mainly built between the wars of the 20th century.

When the Domesday Book was compiled in 1086, Chesterfield was one of six hamlets within the royal manor of Newbold, the others being Whittington, Brimington, Tapton, Boythorpe and Eckington. The chapel at Newbold was almost certainly the mother church for Chesterfield.

By the late twelfth century Chesterfield had outstripped Newbold to become the major market town of north-east Derbyshire. The original market appears to have been located near the parish church, but in 1199 a new market was laid out on the western edge of the town. An indication of Chesterfield's growing importance is the fact that both market sites appear to have operated side-by-side well into the 13th century, but which time leather working, tanning and the manufacture of woollen cloth were all established trades in the town.

Prominent in this view of Holywell Street (below) is the Odeon Cinema, Theatre and Ballroom, which at the time of this photograph was showing Peter Sellers in 'The Battle of the Sexes'. The Odeon is now the Winding Wheel Theatre - named in tribute to the town's coal mining tradition.

CHESTERFIELD, HOLYWELL STREET c1955 C83041

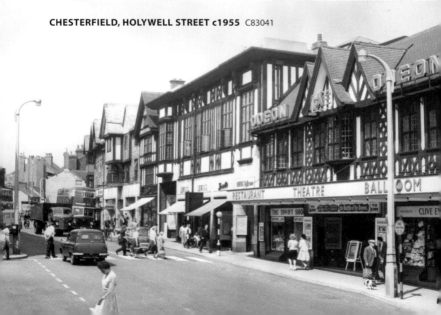

CHESTERFIELD, STEPHENSON PLACE 1914 67563

This photograph shows Stephenson Place, which was named after George Stephenson. He was the engineer responsible for routing the North Midland Railway through Chesterfield. Stephenson married the daughter of a local farmer and spent the last years of his life living at Tapton House near Chesterfield (see page 12), and he died there in 1848. He was interred at Holy Trinity Church beneath the altar, and a stained-glass east window was installed in the church in his memory (see photograph 67568, page 13). A statue of Stephenson was erected outside the town's railway station in 2006. The large round building in this photograph was William Deacon's Bank.

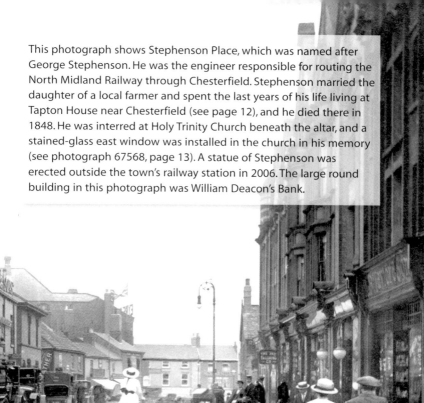

CHESTERFIELD, TAPTON HOUSE 1902 48900

Built in the 18th century, Tapton House is where the railway engineer and businessman George Stephenson spent the last years of his life (photograph 48900, above). Stephenson discovered top grade coking coal at Clay Cross, and the company he founded became known as the Clay Cross Co.

King John, by his charter of 1204, granted a weekly market at Chesterfield, on Saturday, and a fair for eight days at the festival of the Holy Rood. The market at Chesterfield was for corn (particularly wheat and oats), and all kinds of provisions. A later charter of 1631 granted four fairs a year, on February 28th, May 4th (for two days), July 4th and September 14th (for eight days). The February fair was mainly for horses, and the September, or Michaelmas, fair was particularly known for produce such as cheese, apples and onions.

The Guild of St Mary was founded in 1218 to protect privileges granted to Chesterfield by King John. It grew to become a powerful organisation within the town, and there was intense rivalry between wealthy local families for membership. One of the Guild's rules was: 'Each brother shall bequeath in his will, towards masses for the souls of his brethren, twelve pence out of every pound of his chattels; but he need not bequeath more than forty shillings in all'.

CHESTERFIELD, HOLY TRINITY CHURCH, THE GEORGE STEPHENSON MEMORIAL 1914 67568

Chesterfield was badly affected by an outbreak of plague in 1587, but another communicable disease was well-known to the inhabitants of the town in the Middle Ages - leprosy. Like many other boroughs, Chesterfield had a hospital for lepers - St Leonard's - situated at Spital near the Rother, about half a mile to the south-east of the town. Lepers were required to wear something akin to a monk's habit. They carried a cup for the collection of alms and a clapper to warn others that they were near. The rules of the local and powerful Guild of St Mary, founded in 1218, mention leprosy, showing that it was not an uncommon affliction: 'If a brother, through age, or loss of limb, or leprosy, comes to so great a want that he cannot support himself, the brethren who are able shall in turn supply him with needful food ....'

Chesterfield's early industries included leather working, and among the town's products were leather 'jacks', large liquor jugs made from waxed leather and coated on the outside with tar to make them watertight. In medieval times the leather workers often carried out all the processes themselves, stripping the skin, curing, stretching and dyeing. Their workshops would have smelled very unpleasant, as dung was used in some processes and urine in others. Tanning became an industry in its own right; more than one local will from the Chesterfield area refers to items such as the 'netting toobe', 'sorry dog skins', 'white leather' and so on. 'Netting' is an old Derbyshire word for urine and the 'toobe' was the tun where tanners used to store it. 'White leather' was horse skin cured with lime - this kind of skin was quite tough and was often used for making laces and parchment. 'Sorry dog skins', on the other hand, were poor quality skins, including those of dogs, as in medieval England the word sorry also meant 'of little value'.

Around 1278, Chesterfield merchants were able to grab a larger share of the lucrative market in lead at Derby's expense, thanks to the monks of Dale Abbey, who obstructed the navigable Derwent with weirs at Borrowash. Chesterfield was able to offer an alternative route to London and the Continent via the port of Bawtry on the River Idle. For several centuries Chesterfield Fair was one of the most important markets in the country for the buying and selling of lead.

CHESTERFIELD, HIGH STREET 1952 C83004

CHESTERFIELD, MIDLAND STATION
1896 37795a

Photograph 37795a (above) is a general view of Chesterfield from the east. Prominent in the middle distance is the Midland Railway Company's station, recently completely re-built and modernised, and beyond that rise the tower of the Town Hall and the famous twisted spire of the parish church. The history of Derbyshire's main line railways began in the 1830s, and in 1835 the North Midland Railway issued its prospectus for an ambitious scheme for a rail link between Leeds and Derby. George and Robert Stephenson were appointed joint engineers, George playing an active role in promoting the company whilst at the same time amassing considerable business interests along the route, including coal mines at Clay Cross and lime quarries at Ambergate. Also in 1835 the Midland Counties Railway proposed to extend their line from Pinxton to connect with the NMR at either Chesterfield or Clay Cross. The original NMR station at Chesterfield was designed in the Jacobean style by Francis Thompson; it was the largest intermediate station between Derby and Leeds, although it had a relatively short life, being replaced in 1870.

With locally available supplies of iron ore, coal and water, iron-making was also an important industry in the Chesterfield area from the 16th century. Local iron-making received a boost in the 1770s when John Smith took over a furnace, foundry, forge and boring mill at Brampton with the intention of getting into the growing market for castings, especially for steam engines. The Smiths came from Sheffield, where the family had been involved in the cutlery trade. The Brampton site was renamed the Griffin Works. The outbreak of the American War of Independence in 1775 saw the Griffin Works switch more to the production of armaments, especially cannon. This led Smith to open the Adelphi Works as a munitions plant, manufacturing cannonballs and shells for the army and the East India Company. The Smiths enhanced the quality of Derbyshire iron founding by introducing coke-fired blast furnaces into the county. The iron industry would be further boosted by the opening of the Chesterfield Canal in 1777, of which the Adelphi had its own branch.

CHESTERFIELD, MARKET PLACE
1902 48883

17

CHESTERFIELD, MEMORIAL CROSS
1919 69221

The coming of the railways in the 1830s was a further boost to local industries. The Clay Cross Co were the first to send coal to London by rail, and in 1846 the Earl of Stanhope granted Benjamin and Josiah Smith a lease for ironstone, coal and fireclay in the parishes of Dale and Stanton-by-Dale. In 1877 the company founded by Benjamin and Josiah became Stanton Ironworks Co. Sheepbridge Coal & Iron was founded in 1855, and in 1889 Markhams took over the already established firm of Olivers. In 1903 Bryan Donkin & Co relocated to Chesterfield, and three years later the Chesterfield Tube Co also opened for business.

The Chesterfield Canal is one of the earliest in England, the survey having been undertaken by James Brindley in 1768. Construction work began in 1771 at Norwood, where Brindley and his assistant engineer John Varley were faced with the task of driving a 2,893-yard-long tunnel and building a unique flight of thirteen locks split into four groups. The tunnel was officially opened in May 1775, and the canal opened in June 1777. The principle traffic on the canal was coal, though considerable tonnages of stone, lime, timber, lead, iron and corn were also carried. In 1845, in order to compete with the railways, the canal company formed its own railway, but this soon merged as the Manchester, Sheffield & Lincolnshire Railway. Under railway control, the canal remained reasonably prosperous until the late 19th century, but traffic was declining. However, disaster struck in October 1907 when the roof of Norwood tunnel collapsed. The railway company could not justify the expense of rebuilding it, and the section of the canal between the tunnel and Chesterfield was abandoned.

During the 18th century, improvements to the road network in north east Derbyshire were carried out. A number of the turnpikes, such as the Ashover-Chesterfield-Mansfield road, were promoted by the likes of the London Lead Co, and by the 1830s there were fifteen stage and mail coaches a day operating through Chesterfield. The 'Tally Ho' operated the run from Newark to Manchester via Mansfield, Chesterfield, Bakewell, Buxton and New Mills. The 'Telegraph' ran on the Sheffield, Chesterfield, Alfreton, Belper, Derby and Ashbourne route; and the 'Royal Hope' linked the town with Halifax, Huddersfield, Nottingham, Leicester and London.

CHESTERFIELD, QUEEN'S PARK LAKE 1914 67571

CHESTERFIELD, QUEEN'S PARK 1902 48895

The last major railway scheme of the 1890s in north-east Derbyshire was the grandly titled Lancashire, Derbyshire & East Coast Railway which, owing to lack of investment and opposition from existing lines, never got anywhere near Lancashire or the East Coast. However, the LD & ECR's principal feat of engineering is the 700ft long Chesterfield Viaduct, built to carry the line east over the River Hipper. Despite experiencing major problems with Bolsover Tunnel the line opened in 1897, giving Chesterfield its third railway station.

Photograph 37801 (below) shows a view along High Street, with the cobbled Market Place on the right and Scales & Salter's boot and shoe shop on the left; the site of this building was later to house a branch of the Midland Bank. The building next to Salter's was demolished and replaced by a grand three-storey affair housing T Spencer & Co.

Across the street next to Roper and Son is Taylor's drapery store, in the days before it sported the gilt sign seen in photograph 48884 on page 24.

CHESTERFIELD, HIGH STREET 1896 37801

CHESTERFIELD, SCALES & SALTER, HIGH STREET 1896 37801x

On the left of photograph 48884 (below) is the Post Office and the Angel Hotel, which was destroyed by fire in 1917. For those of you with a monetary bent, an 'angel' was an English gold coin, so called for having as its device the Archangel Michael. Its value varied over the years from 6 shillings and 8 pence to 10 shillings. On the right of the photograph, Taylor Bros, the general drapers, have recently invested in a large gilt sign - compare this view with the sign-less shop in photograph 37801 on page 22.

CHESTERFIELD, HIGH STREET 1902 48884

CHESTERFIELD, STEPHENSON MEMORIAL HALL 1902 48890

Mary, Queen of Scots is believed to have stayed at the Angel Hotel in Chesterfield during her long period of captivity by Queen Elizabeth I.

Situated at the head of Corporation Street is the Stephenson Memorial Hall (photograph 48890, above), designed in the plain Gothic style. Originally it housed the Chesterfield & Brampton Mechanics' Institute and the Chesterfield & Derbyshire Institute of Mining, Civil & Mechanical Engineers, and there was also a library, a public hall, some lecture rooms and a laboratory. Nowadays it is also the home of the Pomegranate Theatre.

The traveller and writer Daniel Defoe visited Chesterfield in the 1720s, and was very impressed with the place, describing it as 'a handsome, populous town, well built and well inhabited'. Another traveller, Celia Fiennes, also commented on the town when she visited in 1697:

'Here we Entred Darbyshire and went to Chesterffield 6 mile, and Came by ye Coale mines where they were digging. They make their mines at ye Entrance Like a Well and so till they Come to ye Coale, then they digg all the Ground about where there is Coale and set pillars to support it, and so bring it to ye well where by a basket Like a hand barrow by Cords they pull it up - so they Let down and up the miners with a Cord. Chesterffield Looks Low when you approach it from the Adjacent hill wch you descend, but then you ascend another to it. The Coale pitts and quaraes of stone are all about, Even just at ye town End, and in the town its all built of stone. Ye Church stands in a place of Eminency, the town Looks well, the Streets good, ye Market very Large. It was Satturday wch is their market day and there was a great Market Like some little ffaire, a great deale of Corne and all sorts of ware and ffowles there. I bought my self 2 very good ffatt white (pullings as they Call them) pullets for 6 pence both, and I am sure they were as Large and as good as would have Cost 18 pence if not 2 shills a piece in London-so said all my Company. In this town is ye best ale in the Kingdom Generally Esteem'd.'

The Revolution House at Old Whittington near Chesterfield (below) was formerly the Cock and Pynot Inn. In 1688 it was here that the 4th Earl of Devonshire and other conspirators plotted the overthrow of the Catholic King James II and his replacement with the king's Protestant daughter, Mary, and her Dutch husband, William of Orange.

OLD WHITTINGTON, REVOLUTION HOUSE 1902 48902

27

Five miles east of Chesterfield is the small mining town of Bolsover, whose main employers were the local colliery and coalite works. On a wooded hill above the town stands Bolsover Castle. There was a fortress here in Norman times, but the present buildings date from 1613. The present castle was built by Sir Charles Cavendish, father of the first Duke of Newcastle. Though it looks like a fortress, Bolsover was built as a magnificent stately home; it is thought Sir Charles was trying to recreate a medieval atmosphere. The castle has a superb indoor riding school, and rooms with names such as the Heaven Room and the Star Chamber. King Charles I was a visitor here, and one three-day visit by the king in 1634 is said to have cost his host £15,000, a phenomenal amount of money in 17th-century England.

BOLSOVER, THE CASTLE 1902 48905

CHESTERFIELD, TOWN HALL c1950 C83008

The well kept gardens and fine central portico, supported on six columns, lend a touch of class to the bulk of Chesterfield's Town Hall, seen in photograph C83008, above. It was designed by Bradshaw, Gass & Hope and built between 1937 and 1938.

Chesterfield was the first town in Derbyshire to have electric street lighting, which was installed in 1881.

CHESTERFIELD, THE ROYAL OAK, OLDEST INN
c1960 C83032

STONES
CANNON
ALES

The Royal Oak is the town's oldest inn, shown in photograph C83032, left. It was first recorded as an inn in 1722, but in medieval times there was a rest house here for the Knights Templar, an order of Crusaders. Another old inn, the Peacock, was already scheduled for demolition when it caught fire in 1974. Beneath the Victorian frontage was discovered a timber-framed building - the Peacock was far older than had been thought. The fight against the wholesale demolition of the area lasted long enough for the Peacock to be saved, and it is now the town's tourist information and heritage centre.

During the Napoleonic Wars, Chesterfield accommodated French prisoners of war. They were allowed out during the day, and were summoned back to their quarters in the evening by the ringing of a curfew bell from the church of St Mary and All Saints. During this time, Sir Thomas Hunloke of Wingerworth Hall invited the prisoners of war to use the Roman Catholic chapel at the hall. Technically, Wingerworth was on the wrong side of a milestone which marked the limit of the prisoners' freedom, but Sir Charles solved the problem by having the stone moved!

CHESTERFIELD, HOLYWELL STREET 1954 C83019

The chapel of St Thomas once stood on Holywell Street, but even in the 1830s it was little more than a ruin, much of its stone having been taken for other buildings. Another lost chapel is one thought to have been dedicated to St James at Lord's Mill Bridge, of which no trace remains.

Chesterfield's Italianate, red brick Market Hall (seen in 48882, below) was designed by Davies & Sons and completed in 1857 at a cost of around £8,000. Included in the original structure was a corn exchange, library, mechanics' institute and a magistrates' court. In the 1960s and 70s the Borough Council planned to demolish the Market Hall, New Square and the Shambles and sweep away the open market so that the area could be redeveloped. The plan was for a covered retail area embracing 80 shops topped off with a five-storey office block.

CHESTERFIELD, MARKET PLACE 1902 48882

In the tour guides of the late 19th and early 20th century, the Portland Hotel in Chesterfield was 'well spoken of', with rooms from 3s 6d and lunch for 2s 6d. The Portland was considered to be equal to, if not better than, the Station Hotel; a rare accolade indeed when Britain's railway-operated hotels were amongst the best in the country.

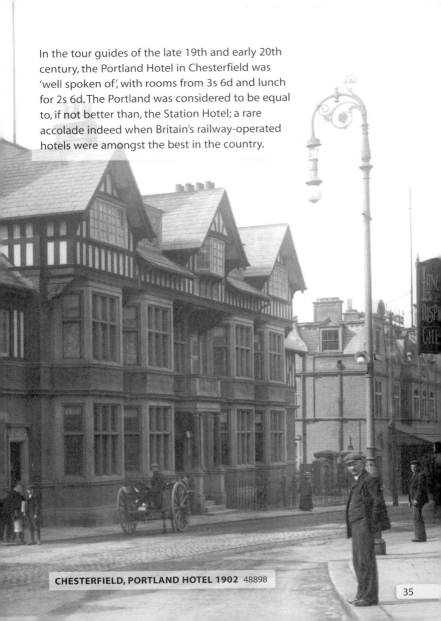

CHESTERFIELD, PORTLAND HOTEL 1902 48898

The lead-covered timber spire of St Mary and All Saints' Parish Church is 228ft high, and leans out of true some 6ft to the south and over 4ft to the west. The famous twisting spire is still moving! Although the spire looks as if it will collapse at any second, it has a very low centre of gravity and is therefore quite safe.

The lady chapel of St Mary and All Saints' Parish Church contains a fine series of alabaster tombs of the Foljambe family, after whom Foljambe Road and Foljambe Avenue are named. One of the most noteworthy of the tombs is that of Sir Godfrey Foljambe, who died in 1541, and his wife, Katharine.

CHESTERFIELD, ST MARY AND ALL SAINTS PARISH CHURCH 1914 67565

CHESTERFIELD, HIGH STREET c1955 C83021

The post-war years saw the spread of high-street chains, and Chesterfield was no exception. In this picture we can see local branches of Timsons, Alexander, Burtons and Boots. Just beyond Boots is Irongate, a part of the old town, with its medieval pattern of narrow lanes and alleyways. Threatened with demolition in the 1960s, the Shambles was saved and rehabilitated in the 1970s.

CHESTERFIELD, QUEEN'S PARK 1902 48894

SPORTING CHESTERFIELD

In August 1874, Derbyshire Cricket Club played Lancashire at Chesterfield, using Chesterfield FC's facilities at Saltergate recreation ground. On becoming a first-class side in 1895, Derbyshire's home games were confined to the County Ground in Derby. With the opening of a cricket pavilion at Queen's Park, Derbyshire CCC returned to Chesterfield in July 1898 with a match against Surrey. In the 1970s Derbyshire CCC temporarily ceased playing at Derby and the club gave serious consideration to a permanent move to Chesterfield. Proposals were drawn up for a new pavilion, indoor nets and a banqueting suite at Queen's Park, but were turned down by Chesterfield Borough Council.

Chesterfield's football team is known 'The Spireites', a reference to the famous twisted spire of the town's parish church. In 1997 the club reached the semi-final of the FA Cup, taking Middlesbrough to a replay following a 3-3 draw. The Spireites lost the replay due to a controversial decision by the referee when he disallowed a Chesterfield goal, a decision that proved to be incorrect following a video replay. If the goal had been allowed, Chesterfield would have progressed to the FA Cup Final, a feat which no other club in the third tier has yet achieved. Perhaps Chesterfield FC's finest hour was in 2006, when the club beat both Manchester City and West Ham United to reach the last 16 of the Carling Cup.

Gordon Banks, the goalkeeper of England's 1966 World Cup-winning team, played for Chesterfield Football Club between 1955 and 1959.

Chesterfield Races dated back to the late 17th century, when they were set up by the first Duke of Devonshire, and were run over a two-mile course encompassing the whole of Whittington Moor and Newbold Moor. The races became less frequent by the end of the 19th century, and finally ceased in 1924, when the last race was run.

CHESTERFIELD, THE CRICKET GROUND, QUEENS PARK c1950 C83009

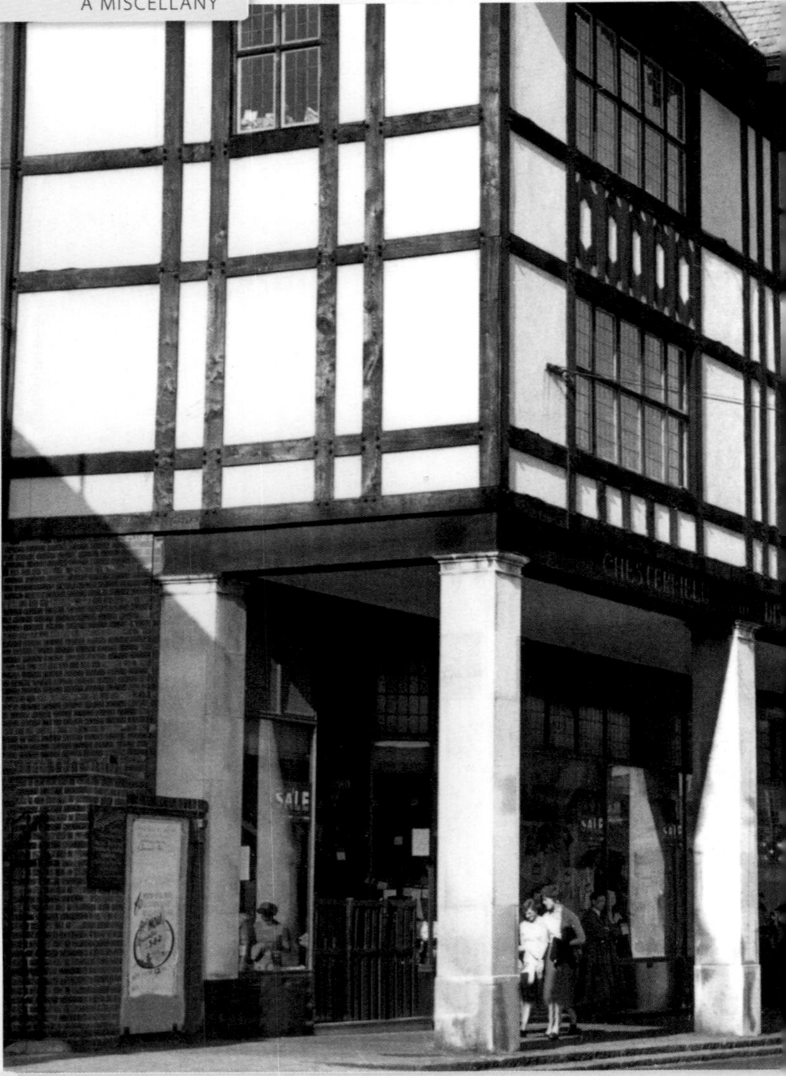
CHESTERFIELD
SALE

CHESTERFIELD, KNIFESMITHGATE c1955 C83022

QUIZ QUESTIONS

Answers on page 50.

1. In medieval times Chesterfield was an important centre for the trading of lead. Lead was produced in 'bole hills' - what were these?

2. Chesterfield's most famous icon is the twisted spire of its parish church of St Mary and All Saints. The twisting is thought to have been caused by the heat of the sun on the lead plates of the roof, which in turn warped the unseasoned timber that had been used in the spire's construction at the end of the 13th century. But what, in folklore, was the traditional explanation for the twisted spire?

3. The medieval heart of old Chesterfield is the narrow-laned area known as the Shambles. What did the name 'Shambles' originally mean?

4. Photograph 48902 on page 27 shows what is now known as the Revolution House at Old Whittington, a few miles from Chesterfield. It was originally the Cock and Pynot Inn - Pynot is an old Derbyshire word for … what?

5. What does the name 'Chesterfield' mean?

6. The Battle of Chesterfield was fought in 1266 between the supporters of Henry III and the barons who had rebelled under Simon de Montfort. After the fighting, where in Chesterfield did Robert de Ferrers, Earl of Derby, try to hide?

7. Which historic item from Chesterfield's past can be found in St Mary and All Saints' churchyard?

8. Several place names in Chesterfield end in the word 'gate', such as Saltergate and Knifesmithgate. This derives from the Danish word 'gata' for street, and is an indication either of the occupations of the local inhabitants or the use of the street in former times, for instance Saltergate was where salt was brought in from Cheshire. Who lived in the street known as Glumangate in medieval times?

9. Queen's Park was originally laid out to offer the town's population of over 27,000 somewhere to go, away from the soot and the grime. But why is Queen's Park so named?

10. What is known as 'A System of Support and Balance', and where in Chesterfield can you find it?

CHESTERFIELD, ST MARY AND ALL SAINTS PARISH CHURCH 1902 48888

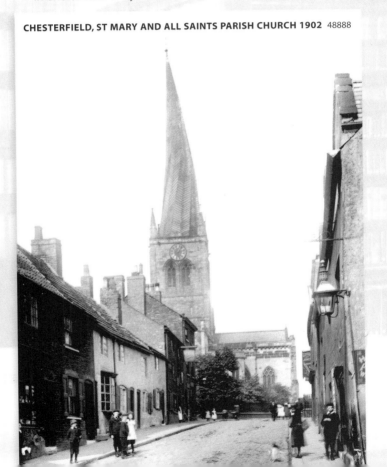

RECIPE

DERBYSHIRE STUFFED ONIONS

In former times onions were traded at Chesterfield's Michaelmas Fair in September.

Ingredients

4 large onions

50g/2oz fresh breadcrumbs

50g/2oz bacon, finely chopped

1 teaspoonful of sage, finely chopped

Salt and pepper to taste

25g/1oz butter

25g/1oz grated cheese

A little chopped fresh parsley to garnish

Remove the onion skins, but keep the onions whole. Place the onions in a large pan of boiling water, and boil for 20 minutes until they are softened.

Preheat the oven to 200°C/400°F/Gas Mark 6.

Remove the onions from the pan and drain, then leave to cool for a few minutes. Cut off the top of each onion, then scoop out the centre and finely chop. Mix together the chopped cooked onions, breadcrumbs, bacon and sage, and season to taste, then mix in the butter well. Use the mixture to fill each onion shell, and sprinkle the tops with the grated cheese. Stand the onions on a baking tray, and bake in the preheated oven for about 30 minutes. Serve garnished with the chopped parsley.

RECIPE

DERBYSHIRE PARKIN

Ingredients

450g/1lb oatmeal

225g/8oz plain flour

100g/4oz butter or margarine

225g/8oz black treacle

225g/8oz golden syrup

50g/2oz soft brown sugar

75g/3oz candied peel and lemon rind

½ teaspoonful of baking powder

A good pinch of ground allspice

Preheat the oven to 190°C/375°F/Gas Mark 5.

Mix together the oatmeal and flour, and rub in the butter or margarine. Add the treacle, golden syrup, sugar, candied peel, lemon peel, baking powder and allspice. Mix together, adding a little warmed water if necessary. Knead the mixture so that all the ingredients are well mixed in.

Grease a deep baking tin, and pour in the mixture - the cooked parkin should be about 5cm (2 inches) thick. Place in the preheated oven and bake for 1-1½ hours. When cooked, cut the parkin into squares and leave in the tin to cool.

Store in an airtight container. Parkin is best left for several days before eating.

CHESTERFIELD, POLICEMEN c1960 C83038x

QUIZ ANSWERS

Questions on page 44.

1. A 'bole hill' was in effect a wind assisted lead smelter. It was a walled enclosure a few feet in diameter, with an opening facing the prevailing wind. It was filled with layers of timber or peat, and then with lead ore. This was covered with more timber, then another layer of ore, and so on until it was full, at which point it was topped off with turf. A channel ran from inside the bole to a gathering pool into which the molten lead would trickle. When the wind was in the right direction the bole was fired, and the smelted ore collected in the gathering pool formed a 'pig' of lead.

2. There are actually many traditional tales about how the church came by its famous twisted spire. One says that a magician managed to persuade a blacksmith in Bolsover to shoe the Devil's cloven hooves. After he drove the first nail into the Devil's foot, the Devil howled in pain and took flight, and lashed out in agony as he flew over Chesterfield, catching the spire with his foot and causing it to twist round. Another version says that the tower buckled under the Devil's weight when he sat on it. There are also two other traditions, neither of which is very complimentary to Chesterfield's inhabitants! One tells how the Devil visited Chesterfield one day and sat on the top of the church spire so that he could have a good look at the place. As it was windy, Old Nick twisted his tail around the spire to prevent himself from falling. When he heard a local person speaking the truth he was so surprised and shocked that he flew off in a hurry without unwinding his tail, causing the spire to twist. The other tells how the spire itself was so amazed to hear that a virgin was being married in the church that it twisted round in an effort

to see this wonder for itself. According to this tale, the spire will straighten itself up again should such a rare event ever occur again!

3. The word 'shambles' comes from the Old English 'shamel', which means a bench or a stall, and in medieval Chesterfield this was the area where the butchers prepared and sold meat from such 'shambles'. The narrowness of the streets also kept the shops cool in the days before refrigeration, and prevented direct sunlight from reaching the meat, helping to preserve it in saleable condition.

4. 'Pynot' is an old Derbyshire word for a magpie.

5. 'Caester' was the Anglo-Saxon word for a Roman fort, and 'feld' meant 'a field where animals graze'. The Anglo-Saxons therefore named the area 'Caester feld', meaning 'the open field near a Roman fort', which eventually became Chesterfield.

6. Robert de Ferrers, Earl of Derby, hid in the parish church of St Mary and All Saints behind some sacks of wool left by traders at the Whitsuntide fair (at this time it was quite usual for churches to also be used as warehouses). Ferrers was betrayed, captured and taken to Windsor in irons.

7. In the churchyard stands Chesterfield's first gas lamp, dating from 1824. It originally stood in the market place.

8. In medieval times Glumangate was where gleemen - or minstrels - lived.

9. Queen's Park was laid out to commemorate Queen Victoria's Golden Jubilee in 1887. The park was opened in 1893.

10. 'A System of Support and Balance' is the name of an artwork by Paul Lewthwaite which stands outside Chesterfield Magistrates' Court.

Did You Know?
CHESTERFIELD
A MISCELLANY

SWALLOWS

FRANCIS FRITH

PIONEER VICTORIAN PHOTOGRAPHER

Francis Frith, founder of the world-famous photographic archive, was a complex and multi-talented man. A devout Quaker and a highly successful Victorian businessman, he was philosophical by nature and pioneering in outlook. By 1855 he had already established a wholesale grocery business in Liverpool, and sold it for the astonishing sum of £200,000, which is the equivalent today of over £15,000,000. Now in his thirties, and captivated by the new science of photography, Frith set out on a series of pioneering journeys up the Nile and to the Near East.

INTRIGUE AND EXPLORATION

He was the first photographer to venture beyond the sixth cataract of the Nile. Africa was still the mysterious 'Dark Continent', and Stanley and Livingstone's historic meeting was a decade into the future. The conditions for picture taking confound belief. He laboured for hours in his wicker dark-room in the sweltering heat of the desert, while the volatile chemicals fizzed dangerously in their trays. Back in London he exhibited his photographs and was 'rapturously cheered' by members of the Royal Society. His reputation as a photographer was made overnight.

VENTURE OF A LIFE-TIME

By the 1870s the railways had threaded their way across the country, and Bank Holidays and half-day Saturdays had been made obligatory by Act of Parliament. All of a sudden the working man and his family were able to enjoy days out, take holidays, and see a little more of the world.

With typical business acumen, Francis Frith foresaw that these new tourists would enjoy having souvenirs to commemorate their days out. For the next thirty years he travelled the country by train and by pony and trap, producing fine photographs of seaside resorts and beauty spots that were keenly bought by millions of Victorians. These prints were painstakingly pasted into family albums and pored over during the dark nights of winter, rekindling precious memories of summer excursions. Frith's studio was soon supplying retail shops all over the country, and by 1890 F Frith & Co had become the greatest specialist photographic publishing company in the world, with over 2,000 sales outlets, and pioneered the picture postcard.

FRANCIS FRITH'S LEGACY

Francis Frith had died in 1898 at his villa in Cannes, his great project still growing. By 1970 the archive he created contained over a third of a million pictures showing 7,000 British towns and villages.

Frith's legacy to us today is of immense significance and value, for the magnificent archive of evocative photographs he created provides a unique record of change in the cities, towns and villages throughout Britain over a century and more. Frith and his fellow studio photographers revisited locations many times down the years to update their views, compiling for us an enthralling and colourful pageant of British life and character.

We are fortunate that Frith was dedicated to recording the minutiae of everyday life. For it is this sheer wealth of visual data, the painstaking chronicle of changes in dress, transport, street layouts, buildings, housing and landscape that captivates us so much today, offering us a powerful link with the past and with the lives of our ancestors.

Computers have now made it possible for Frith's many thousands of images to be accessed almost instantly. The archive offers every one of us an opportunity to examine the places where we and our families have lived and worked down the years. Its images, depicting our shared past, are now bringing pleasure and enlightenment to millions around the world a century and more after his death.

For further information visit: www.francisfrith.com

INTERIOR DECORATION

Frith's photographs can be seen framed and as giant wall murals in thousands of pubs, restaurants, hotels, banks, retail stores and other public buildings throughout Britain. These provide interesting and attractive décor, generating strong local interest and acting as a powerful reminder of gentler days in our increasingly busy and frenetic world.

FRITH PRODUCTS

All Frith photographs are available as prints and posters in a variety of different sizes and styles. In the UK we also offer a range of other gift and stationery products illustrated with Frith photographs, although many of these are not available for delivery outside the UK – see our web site for more information on the products available for delivery in your country.

THE INTERNET

Over 100,000 photographs of Britain can be viewed and purchased on the Frith web site. The web site also includes memories and reminiscences contributed by our customers, who have personal knowledge of localities and of the people and properties depicted in Frith photographs. If you wish to learn more about a specific town or village you may find these reminiscences fascinating to browse. Why not add your own comments if you think they would be of interest to others? See **www.francisfrith.com**

PLEASE HELP US BRING FRITH'S PHOTOGRAPHS TO LIFE

Our authors do their best to recount the history of the places they write about. They give insights into how particular towns and villages developed, they describe the architecture of streets and buildings, and they discuss the lives of famous people who lived there. But however knowledgeable our authors are, the story they tell is necessarily incomplete.

Frith's photographs are so much more than plain historical documents. They are living proofs of the flow of human life down the generations. They show real people at real moments in history; and each of those people is the son or daughter of someone, the brother or sister, aunt or uncle, grandfather or grandmother of someone else. All of them lived, worked and played in the streets depicted in Frith's photographs.

We would be grateful if you would give us your insights into the places shown in our photographs: the streets and buildings, the shops, businesses and industries. Post your memories of life in those streets on the Frith website: what it was like growing up there, who ran the local shop and what shopping was like years ago; if your workplace is shown tell us about your working day and what the building is used for now. Read other visitors' memories and reconnect with your shared local history and heritage. With your help more and more Frith photographs can be brought to life, and vital memories preserved for posterity, and for the benefit of historians in the future.

Wherever possible, we will try to include some of your comments in future editions of our books. Moreover, if you spot errors in dates, titles or other facts, please let us know, because our archive records are not always completely accurate—they rely on 140 years of human endeavour and hand-compiled records. You can email us using the contact form on the website.

Thank you!

For further information, trade, or author enquiries
please contact us at the address below:

**The Francis Frith Collection, Oakley Business Park,
Wylye Road, Dinton, Wiltshire SP3 5EU England.**
Tel: +44 (0)1722 716 376 Fax: +44 (0)1722 716 881
e-mail: sales@francisfrith.co.uk **www.francisfrith.com**